Growing up
ISLAM

Janet Ardavan

Series editor: Jean Holm

What is this book about?

One of the most interesting ways to learn about a religion is to try to see it through the eyes of children who are growing up in a religious family. In this way we can discover something of what it *feels* like to belong to the religion.

In the books in this series we shall be finding out how children gradually come to understand the real meaning of the festivals they celebrate, the scriptures and other stories they hear, the ceremonies they take part in, the symbols of their religion and the customs and traditions of their religious community. This should provide a good foundation for going on to a wider study of the religions.

The five books in this series deal with the main religions that are found in Britain today: Christianity, Hinduism, Islam, Judaism and Sikhism. However, some things are more important in one religion than in another. For example, festivals play a bigger part in the lives of Jewish children than they do in the lives of Sikh children, and the scriptures play a bigger part in the lives of Muslim children than they do in the lives of Hindu children, so although many of the same topics are dealt with in all the books, the pattern of each book is slightly different.

There are differences within every religion as well as between religions, and even a very long book could not describe the customs and beliefs of all the groups that make up a religion. In these books we may be learning more about one of the groups, or traditions, within the religion, but there will be references to the different ways in which other groups practise their faith.

In this series of books we are using BCE (Before the Christian Era) and CE (in the Christian Era) instead of BC and AD, which refer to Christian beliefs about the significance of Jesus.

How to use this book

Some of you will be studying religions for the first time. Others may already have learnt something about places of worship or festivals, and you will be able to gain greater understanding and fit what you know into a wider picture of the religion.

As you learn about how children grow up in a religion, prepare a display, or perhaps make a large class book. You will find some suggestions of activities in the text, but you will be able to think of many more. If your display is good enough it might be possible to put it up in the hall or in a corridor so that lots of people can see it. Try to show what it feels like to be on the 'inside' of the religion, so that other pupils and teachers and visitors to the school will be able to learn about the religion from the point of view of the children who are growing up in it.

Contents

Ways to worship — 4
Learning to live as a Muslim — 4
Learning the Qur'an — 4
Writing Arabic — 6
The giving of the Qur'an — 10
Learning to pray — 12
The Shahada — 20
The mosque — 21

Fasting, festivals and food — 26
Fasting — 26
The festival of Eid-al-Fitr — 30
The festival of Eid-al-Adha — 32
The importance of the hajj — 33
Hajj observances — 34
Food laws — 42

Rights and relationships — 44
Relationships between men and women — 44
What parents should do for children — 48
What children should do for parents — 50
Death and after — 52
Relationships with the wider community — 54
Relationships with the natural world — 56
Living a Muslim life — 58

Glossary — 62

Index — 64

The words in the glossary are printed in **bold** type the first time they appear in the book.

# Ways to worship

In the name of God, the compassionate the merciful...

Learning to live as a Muslim

There are Muslim families in almost every country in the world. Muslim children grow up in places as far apart as Britain and China, Nigeria and Indonesia. They may speak different languages, wear different clothes and live in different kinds of homes from each other, but there are certain things that they will all learn as they grow up, because they are all Muslims. In this book, we are going to find out about some of these things.

Learning the Qur'an

*"In our family we all have our own copy of the **Qur'an**. I got my own as soon as I had learned to read some parts from it at mosque school. We keep them up on a special bookshelf in the room where we pray. We treat it very carefully, with very great respect — not so much respect that we don't even read it, of course, but we wouldn't get it dirty or anything like that because these are words straight from God."*

Mosque school

*"I started mosque school when I was five. I used to go for two hours after my ordinary school finished. It was quite hard work learning the alphabet and at first I used to get very tired. But I was proud when I started to learn the **surahs** by heart when I was about six. I felt very grown up. Sometimes the teacher used to tell us stories of the prophets, Prophet Adam and Prophet **Nuh** for example, and I used to enjoy those very much. I left mosque school just before I went to secondary school. By then I had read the Qur'an all the way through and I had learned a lot of the surahs by heart."*

From their earliest years, children can see that the Qur'an is different from other books. They see that it is handled carefully and with respect. They hear the adults in their family reciting passages from it each time they pray and at ceremonies such as weddings and funerals. They may also notice that adults read the Qur'an when they need guidance and help with their daily lives. All these things help children to realise quite early in their lives how important the Qur'an is.

As soon as they are old enough, most children begin to study Arabic so that they can read the Qur'an. If they live in a country where the majority of people are Muslims, such as Iran, Saudi Arabia or Pakistan, they will probably study the Qur'an as part of one of their normal school courses, Islamic Studies. In countries where Islamic Studies are not a normal part of the curriculum, children may go to special classes after school finishes or at weekends. These classes are usually held at the local mosque. Once they have learned the Arabic alphabet, their teacher will help them to begin to read the Qur'an and to understand what it means. Of course, many Muslim children live in countries where Arabic is the national language, for example, countries in North Africa and parts of the Middle East, so these early stages of learning the Qur'an are easier for them, even though there is a difference between the Arabic of the Qur'an and modern spoken Arabic.

As soon as they are familiar with the letters, children begin to learn passages from the Qur'an by heart, starting with those they need to use in their daily prayers. You can read one of the first and most important prayers they learn on page 9. They are expected to learn to recite these passages *exactly* as they are written in the Qur'an — no mistakes at all are allowed and their teacher will be very strict about this! Some people manage to memorise the whole of the Qur'an and this is considered a great achievement. To mark this achievement they may use the title '**Hafiz**' before their name.

Writing Arabic

					غ	ghayn	gh
ا	alif	a	ر	ra	r	ف	fa	f
ب	ba	b	ز	zay	z	ق	qaf	q
ت	ta	t	س	sin	s	ك	kaf	k
ث	tha	th	ش	shin	sh	ل	lam	l
ج	jim	j	ص	sad	s	م	mim	m
ح	ha	h	ض	dad	d	ن	nun	n
خ	kha	kh	ط	ta	t	ه	ha	h
د	dal	d	ظ	za	z	و	waw	w
ذ	dhal	dh	ع	ayn		ي	ya	y

'It was quite hard work learning the alphabet...'

Here is your chance to try some Arabic! This chart shows the letters of the Arabic alphabet as they appear in their printed form in books, newspapers and typewritten material. The name and the sound of each letter is shown too, though of course some of the sounds are not used in English and so they cannot be represented very accurately.

Because of how the letters are joined together, the shape of a letter in Arabic looks slightly different according to whether it comes at the beginning, in the middle or at the end of a word. Some letters never join to the letter that follows. The short vowels (b**a**t, b**i**t, b**u**t) are shown by signs above or below the word, and not by letters as they are in English. There are no capital letters in Arabic.

Let's look at a word to see how this works — don't forget to read and write from right to left!

Here are four letters:

d   m   h   m   ⟵ Start here.

ܕ   ܡ   ܚ   ܡ   ⟵ Read this way.

Take the first section of each of the first three letters to join them together.

d   m   h   m

ܕ ـܡ ـܚ ـܡ

d   m   h   m

ܕܡܚܡ

d m h m

ܡܚܡܕ

Put in the short vowels.

a´   a´   u'

And the sign ܘ which makes a consonant sound double.

Can you read it now?

The Prophet Muhammad

The Prophet Muhammad was born in Makkah in 570 CE. He was a kind and honest man known as 'Al–Amin', the Trustworthy One, at a time when Arab society was corrupt and divided by warfare among the great families. Drinking, gambling and idol worship were common. Muhammad was deeply worried by the corruption within his society, and especially by the idol worship. He did not believe that carved idols made by men could have the slightest influence on people's lives. He believed in one God, the creator of the universe, and would often leave the city to be alone to worship this one God, **Allah**, and think about what people's relationship with God should be. One night, as he was sitting alone thinking, something happened which finally led the people to accept Muhammad as the last Prophet sent by God to people on Earth. You can read about it on page 10.

Nowadays, Muslims read about the life of Muhammad and of his family and try to live their own lives as he did. For them, Muhammad's life is an example which they should all try to follow. When Muslims write or print in a book the name of the Prophet Muhammad, they put the Arabic words which mean, 'may the peace and blessing of Allah be upon him' after the name to show their respect for him. Sometimes in English, the letters p.b.u.h. (peace be upon him) appear instead.

Muḥammad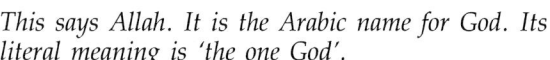

Calligraphy

In the example on the previous page, the letters have been joined together very simply as they would be printed in a book, a typewritten letter or a newspaper. Handwriting is considered to be a very important art form in Islamic cultures and handwritten words often look more complicated and certainly more beautiful than typewritten ones. The art of handwriting is called calligraphy.

This says Allah. It is the Arabic name for God. Its literal meaning is 'the one God'.

Compare the two ways of writing Muhammad. Can you pick out the letters in the calligraphic version?

> Make copies of the calligraphic forms of Allah and Muhammad to add to your class display or to your own book.
>
> You could show underneath which Arabic letters make up the word Muhammad, and how they join together.

Al-Fatihah

Praise be to Allah, Lord of the Worlds,
The beneficent, the Merciful.
Owner of the Day of Judgment,
Thee alone we worship;
Thee alone we ask for help.
Show us the straight path,
The path of those whom thou hast favoured;
not the path of those who earn Thine
anger nor of those who go astray.

*This photograph shows a page from a copy of the Qur'an hand written about four hundred years ago. It is the first surah of the Qur'an, called the **Fatihah** which means the 'Opening'. This is a particularly important surah, one of the first that Muslim children learn by heart and use as a prayer. It is so important that it is sometimes called Ummu'l Qur'an which means 'the essence of the Qur'an'.*

Some of the Prophet's friends described how he looked. Here are some of the things they wrote about him.

Anas ibn Malik says: 'The Prophet of Allah had a moderate stature, being neither very tall nor very short. His person was finely symmetrical and the hair of his head was neither very curly nor very straight; his complexion was tawny.' (Tirmidhi)

Hind says: 'He walked softly and firmly with a rapid pace and a slightly forward bend, as if he were descending from a higher to a lower level. Whenever he looked at anything he would look straight into it; his eyes were always downcast, directed more towards the earth than towards the sky.' (Tirmidhi)

The giving of the Qur'an

Read: In the name of thy Lord Who createth,
Createth man from a clot.
Read: And thy Lord is the Most Bounteous,
Who teacheth by the pen,
Teacheth man that which he knew not. (96: 1−5)

'...these are the words straight from God...'

The Qur'an is treated with such honour and respect because of what it contains and how it came into being. Muslim children are told how the Angel Gabriel appeared to Muhammad one night. Muhammad had gone, as he often did, to the cave on the summit of nearby Mount Hira outside Makkah where he lived, to be alone and to meditate. The angel twice said to Muhammad 'Read!' Twice Muhammad replied 'I cannot read'. But when the angel repeated the order for a third time, Muhammad said 'What shall I read?' Then the angel spoke the words you can see at the top of the page, telling Muhammad that the revelation he was receiving was from God. The words remained sharp in Muhammad's memory.

This was the first of many revelations that Muhammad received from God through the Angel Gabriel during the years that followed. Each time, Muhammad memorised the Arabic words exactly. At first he shared them only with his wife and family and his closest friends but gradually, many people in Makkah came to believe that Muhammad had received a message for all people from God and was a prophet, just as Adam, Abraham, Noah, Jesus and many others had been before him. These friends of Muhammad were the first to call themselves Muslims. They too learned by heart the exact words of the revelations Muhammad had received. These were finally gathered together and written down in the order that had also been described to Muhammad by the angel to form the book known as the Qur'an, which means the 'Recitation'.

God's own words   So, Muslim children learn that the Arabic words of the Qur'an are God's own words.

This explains why Muslims insist that the words should not be changed in any way either when they are spoken or written down. The messages given by God to man through the prophets who came before Muhammad, have, according to the Qur'an, been changed. Their meaning is no longer clear because the original revelations are not present, only translations which are subject to change through time. For Muslims, Muhammad is the last of the prophets and his message is the final and complete one, so it must be passed on exactly as he received it.

The Qur'an

1 Muslims believe that the Qur'an was revealed to the Prophet Muhammad between the years 610 CE and 632 CE, the year of the Prophet's death. Since Muhammad himself, in common with most people of the time, could neither read nor write, he dictated his revelations to a group of close friends as soon as he had received them. All of them memorised the verses as they were revealed. Very soon after Muhammad's death, these writings were gathered together in one volume, which was entrusted to the Prophet's widow for safe keeping. This volume was the model for all other copies of the Qur'an.

2 The Qur'an is divided into 114 surahs or chapters and each surah is divided into **ayahs**. Some surahs have only three ayahs (e.g. surahs 103 and 108) while the longest, surah 2, is made up of 286 ayahs. Each surah has a name which is related to part of its content. When references are given, the first number refers to the surah and the second to the verse.

3 When Muslim children learn surahs from the Qur'an, they do not necessarily learn them in the order in which they appear. This is because the Qur'an does not form a continuous narrative. Muslims say that it should be read little by little and that those who read it should think carefully about what its message is as they read. The real purpose of the Qur'an, they say, is to teach people about God and about their relationship to God. To help them to understand this relationship, the Qur'an offers guidance on every aspect of their lives.

Learning to pray

"My grandma really taught me how to say prayers. I used to watch her when I was very little while she did her prayers in our home. She said her prayers five times a day like you should, but it was easy for her because she was always at home. She didn't mind me watching, but I had to keep quiet and not bother her.

Then one day I started to copy her. I stood up when she stood up, and kneeled when she did, so she said, 'Now you are a big girl. You can learn too', and she showed me what the proper prayer positions are, but first she made me learn **wudu** *because it is very important to be clean for prayers. It means you are ready in your mind to say your prayers and that's important. We always take our outdoor shoes off in the house anyway, to keep it clean, but when she said her prayers my grandma took her slippers off and put a rug on the floor to make a clean place to pray in. So I did too.*

We know which way to face now, because when we first moved in my dad used a compass to find where Makkah is, so now we always know. It took me a long time to learn all the right words, though, and how many **rak'ahs** *to do at different prayer times. I didn't really know all that until I was about ten or so, I think. Some of the words my mum taught me and some I learned at mosque school. Now I say prayers at home with my mum and my sister. We don't usually go to the mosque except at* **Eid**. *My dad goes on Fridays though, and sometimes he takes my little brother."*

Why prayer is important

'She said her prayers five times a day like you should...'

The Qur'an stresses how important it is for Muslims to pray at regular intervals throughout the day. They can pray wherever they happen to be – at home, at work, or even in an airport or railway station. The place is not important, but fulfilling the duty to pray is. One of the friends of Muhammad gave an account of how he once heard the Prophet explaining why it is important for people to pray. The account says that just as a bather is made physically clean by the water, so prayer helps a person to have a pure mind.

'Abu Hurairah reported that he heard the Messenger of Allah (peace and blessings of Allah be on him) say: "Tell me, if there is a stream at the door of one of you in which he bathes five times every day, what dost thou say, will it leave anything of his dirt?" They said, "It would not leave anything of his dirt." He said: "This is the likeness of the five prayers, with which Allah blots out all faults."' (Bukhari)

This account is a **hadith**.

Hadiths

When the Prophet Muhammad was alive, those who knew him paid special attention to everything that he said and did. In later years accounts of his words and actions were gathered together in books of 'hadiths'. 'Hadith' just means 'a saying' or 'a report'. Muslims use these 'reports' of how Muhammad did things as guides for their own actions, because the Qur'an tells them that his is the best example to follow.

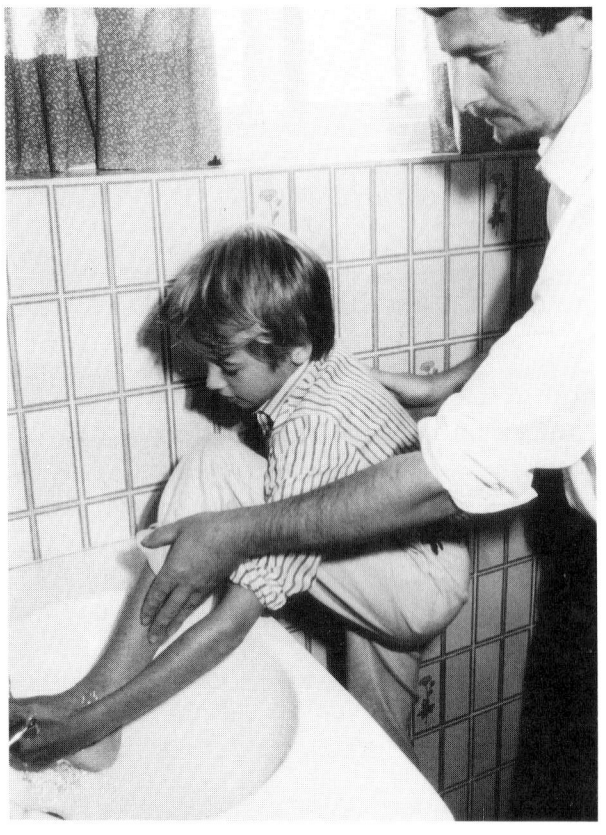

Washing before prayer

'...first she made me learn wudu because it is very important to be clean for prayers.'

Muslims wash before praying. The washing is partly to clean and refresh them before prayer but more important than that, it reminds them once again that their souls need to be purified by prayer just as their bodies are cleaned by water. They wash three times their hands, mouth, nostrils, face, fore arms (right arm first), head, ears, neck and feet — all the parts of their body that are likely to get dusty and dirty as they go about their work. The washing is done in this special order because that was how Muhammad washed before he prayed, according to the accounts given in the hadiths by friends who had known him.

How to do wudu — a story.

There was once in Makkah a scholar famous for his teachings about Islam. One day, there was a great banging at his door. He opened it and saw a ragged looking man with an old, torn blanket around his shoulders. The scholar looked rather disdainfully at him.

'Who are you? What do you want?' he said.

'I want to learn to do wudu,' the ragged man said.

'To do wudu?' said the scholar in astonishment. 'But you are an old man! Has no one ever taught you how to do wudu?'

'Of course,' replied the ragged man. 'My father taught me. But you are a wise man, a great teacher, and I want to learn it from you too.'

So, feeling flattered, the scholar began, rather impatiently, to tell the other how to do wudu. 'First you must wash your hands three times, right hand first, then...'

But the ragged man interrupted him. 'Could you kindly show me instead of just telling me?'

'Show you? Don't you even understand simple language, that you bother me to show you?'

'Yes, I do, but you are a scholar, and I want to see with my own eyes how a wise man like you does wudu.'

So, very impatiently by now, the scholar began to show the ragged man, and as he washed, he explained all that he was doing, asking all the time, 'Are you watching carefully? Are you taking notice? Are you learning?'

When he had finished, there was a pause. Then the ragged man spoke. 'Have you finished? Are you satisfied that you have done your wudu properly?'

'Properly? Properly? I have done it exactly as it is written that we should do it! I am fully satisfied!'

'Very well,' said the ragged man, 'now watch how I do it.' And he began to wash. But instead of washing his hands three times as the scholar had done, he washed four times.

The scholar was furious. 'What?' he shouted. 'I have told you, I have showed you, and still you can't remember! You are rinsing four times!'

'Ah, scholar, it seems you have not been able to teach me properly how to do wudu,' said the ragged man. And he turned and went.

The way he said that made the scholar curious and rather uncomfortable. So he called his servant to follow the ragged man to find out who he was. The servant came back some time later, worried and a little fearful.

'Master,' he said, 'that ragged man was Hatim Asam himself!'

Now Hatim Asam was known throughout the Muslim world for his saintliness and learning and the scholar was ashamed of having treated him so badly. So that night, he went to him and said, 'Master, I am sorry. Please forgive me for my behaviour this morning.'

Hatim Asam said, 'There is no need to ask my forgiveness. But there is something you should understand. When you were trying to teach me about wudu, you were talking all the time. That is wrong. When you do wudu, you should concentrate on that alone. You should be praying to Allah to forgive you whatever sins you have committed. You were not doing wudu, you were just washing. Wudu must be done with concentration and repentence. Remember that.'

Qiyam (standing).

Ruku (bowing the head and body).

Sajdah (prostration).

Jalsah (sitting).

'...a clean place to pray in...'

The idea of a clean place to pray in is once again a reminder that prayer purifies – we have already seen that people should be clean when they pray, and the place they pray in should also be as clean as possible. That is why Muslims often spread a prayer mat on the floor in their own homes when they pray. The prayer mat itself has no importance. They could equally well use any clean cloth, or nothing at all if nothing is available.

The direction of prayer

'...my dad used a compass to find where Makkah is...'

Muslims will always try to pray facing Makkah because the Prophet Muhammad established the tradition of facing the **Ka'aba** when he prayed, after it was revealed to him that he should do so (2:150). Some people own a specially marked compass so that wherever they are, they can always find the direction of Makkah when it is time to pray.

> Look at a world map. Find Britain and Saudi Arabia. In which direction should Muslims in Britain turn in order to face Makkah? What about Muslims who live in Pakistan? Or the USSR? Or Malaysia? Choose four or five countries in different parts of the world and complete the sentence for each one.
>
> Muslims who live in........turn to the........to face the Ka'aba when they pray.
>
> Can you think of a way to show this information on a diagram?

The prayer positions

...she showed me what the proper prayer positions are...'

The photographs show the positions used in each prayer sequence, or rak'ah. Each of the five daily prayer services is made up of two, three or four rak'ahs according to the time of day. As you can see, there are four different positions in worship, all mentioned in different places in the Qur'an and each with a special name. Many different prayers, some prescribed and some chosen by the individual are offered during a service. The Fatihah, the first surah of the Qur'an, and one of the very first prayers Muslim children learn by heart, is an essential part of every rak'ah of every prayer service. The rules governing prayer are very detailed. To follow them closely is part of the discipline of being a Muslim. But just following the rules is not enough. Muslims must understand the significance of what they are saying, and be alert during prayer times. One of the friends of Muhammad reported that the Prophet once said, 'When a person is drowsy in his prayers, let him go to sleep until he knows what he recites'. Muslims believe that prayers are for the good of the worshipper — if people don't know what their prayers mean and are just repeating them in a mechanical way without thinking, the prayers cannot help them to come closer to God.

Prayer is one of the five most important duties of a Muslim.

Time of formal prayers

'...and how many rak'ahs to do at the different prayer times...'

NAME OF PRAYER	TIME OF PRAYER	NUMBER OF RAK'AHS IN PRAYER
maghreb (evening prayers)	some time between sunset and nightfall	three
isha (night prayers)	some time between nightfall and dawn	four
fajr (dawn prayers)	some time between dawn and sunrise	two
zhur (noon prayers)	some time between noon and mid-afternoon	four
asr (afternoon prayers)	some time between mid-afternoon and just before sunset	four

This chart shows the names and times of the five daily prayers and how many rak'ahs make up each one. The Arabic word for prayers is **'salat'** and these prescribed prayers are **'fard'** which means obligatory. Extra rak'ahs may be added to the prescribed number. These non-obligatory prayers are known as **'sunnah'**. The names of the prayers (maghreb, isha, fajr, zhur and asr) are the Arabic words for the time of day when they are said.

All these details about prayer in the last few pages may look rather complicated unless you are a Muslim! But of course, as you can see from the girl's words on page 13, Muslim children don't have to learn it all at once. From the time they are very little they see and hear their family praying and they join in when they are able to. No one expects them to do it perfectly at first but they are expected not to disrupt prayer times. They must not talk or shout while others are praying even if they are not old enough to pray themselves. So they begin to learn to be disciplined about prayer even when they are quite young.

So far we have been learning about formal prayers. But there are many Arabic phrases which are really forms of worship that occur in the everyday conversation of Muslims wherever they live and whatever language they speak. Look on page 4 and you will see that we began this book with one of these phrases.

Prayers in everyday conversation

Bismillah al rahman al rahim بسم الله الرحمن الرحيم
'In the name of God, the compassionate, the merciful.'

Whenever they start something important, Muslims begin by saying 'bismillah'. They may say it before beginning a meal. Teachers starting a lesson may say it. When babies are too young to say it for themselves, their mother will say it for them.

Whenever you are welcomed with a greeting, then answer back with something finer than it, or (at least) return it. God is a Reckoner for everything
Al-Qur'an 4 : 86

When they greet or leave one another, Muslims say:

assalamu aleykum السلام عليكم
Peace be with you.

And the reply is:

wa aleykum salam وعليكم السلام
And peace be with you too.

Another short phrase which is often heard in everyday conversation is:

alhamdullillah الحمد لله
Praise be to God.

This may be said at the end of a meal. For instance, if someone asks, 'How are you?' a Muslim may reply 'alhamdullillah, I am well.' It is a way of acknowledging that everything comes from God and you are grateful for it.

Because these phrases are often used in conversation, little children begin to learn them very early on as part of their everyday language, without even realising that they are forms of worship.

"But really in Islam, prayers are part of everything you do because Islam is a way of life. It affects everything you do. You greet your family in an Islamic way, you say goodbye in an Islamic way, you start your work in an Islamic way. You remember God in everything."

The Shahada

أشهد أنّ لا إله إلا الله
وأشهد أنّ محمّدًا رسول الله

'I bear witness that there is no God but Allah and I bear witness that Muhammad is the messenger (prophet) of Allah.'

This is the **Shahada**, the declaration of faith. It is the centre of the Islamic faith. It forms part of all the prayers and of the **adhan**, the call to prayer. The adhan, then, really serves two purposes. It announces that it is time for prayer, but it also states the most basic principle of Islam — that there is no God but Allah and Muhammad is his prophet. The Arabic word for this basic principle is **tawheed** which means unity.

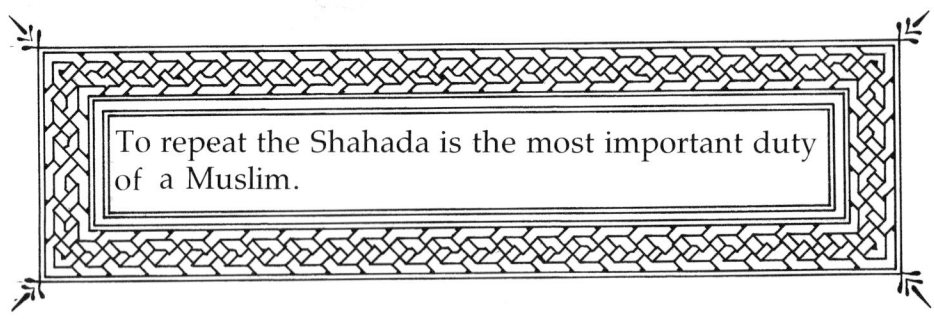

To repeat the Shahada is the most important duty of a Muslim.

The adhan

الله أكبر الله أكبر	Allah is most great Allah is most great
الله أكبر الله أكبر	Allah is most great Allah is most great
أشهد أن لا إله إلا الله	I bear witness that there is no god apart from God
أشهد أن لا إله إلا الله	I bear witness that there is no god apart from God
أشهد أن محمدا رسول الله	I bear witness that Muhammad is God's messenger
أشهد أن محمدا رسول الله	I bear witness that Muhammad is God's messenger
حي على الصلاة	Come to prayer
حي على الصلاة	Come to prayer
حي على الفلاح	Come to Salvation
حي على الفلاح	Come to Salvation
الله أكبر الله أكبر	God is great God is great
لا إله إلا الله	There is no god apart from God.

The mosque

'My dad goes to mosque on Fridays and sometimes he takes my little brother.'

Friday is a special day for Muslims. It is the day when instead of praying at home or at work, they gather together as a community at the mosque for the Friday service, which takes place at the same time as the zhur prayers. In Muslim countries, businesses will be closed for the period of the Friday service, though they may be open for the rest of the day.

It is considered very important for the whole Muslim community to gather together on Fridays. Boys will go to the mosque with their fathers even if they are too young to pray. Women and girls should make a special effort to attend whenever possible, though it is not considered a duty for them to go to the mosque as it is for men and boys. If household duties make it difficult for them to go, they can say the zhur prayers at home as they do on other days. In Britain, the custom among Muslim women varies. In some communities women never go to the mosque. In others they do, especially where the mosque is large enough to offer facilities such as separate washing areas and perhaps a prayer gallery or a separate prayer hall for them.

The call to prayer from the minaret of a mosque in Egypt.

Inside the mosque

Some mosques in Britain are purpose-built and others are in buildings which have been converted from some other use. A purpose-built mosque will probably have a courtyard where people can meet and talk, a dome symbolising the heavens and a minaret from which the **mu'adhdhin** can make the call to prayer, although nowadays the call to prayer is often a tape recording, broadcast through a loud-speaker. A converted mosque will perhaps only be recognisable by its name board. Inside, all the mosques, whether purpose-built or not, will have certain features in common.

"The building that is now our mosque used to be a garage. The people in our community bought it and converted it so we could have an Islamic community centre, somewhere we could pray and have meetings. There are rooms for Qur'an classes, a wash room where we do wudu before prayers and the prayer room.

*In the prayer room there is one special wall. It is called the '***qibla***' wall. If you face that wall you will be facing the Ka'aba in Makkah. It has a sort of alcove in it called the* **mihrab** *to show it's the qibla wall. Also it has quotations from the Qur'an, and the* **minbar** *is against that wall too. The* **imam** *goes up there to do the sermon at Friday prayers. Our minbar looks like three little steps but bigger mosques sometimes have much higher ones. The floor is covered with one big carpet and there's a cupboard by the door with little prayer mats in it that people can get out when they come to pray and they put them back when they have finished. Outside the door there's a metal rack to put shoes in, otherwise all the pairs would get muddled up."*

qibla The direction of the Ka'aba in Makkah. When Muslims pray facing the Ka'aba they know that all other Muslims in the world will be facing the same point. This awareness helps strengthen the feeling of community among Muslims all over the world.

mihrab The mihrab, the niche on the qibla wall, shows the direction of prayer. The design on a prayer rug often includes a representation of a mihrab.

minbar This is the pulpit from which the imam, or prayer leader, delivers his **khutbah** ('speech' or 'sermon') at Friday prayers. It is the addition of the khutbah that makes Friday prayers different from other zhur prayers. The hadiths say that Prophet Muhammad used to take a verse of the Qur'an as a text for his sermons and explain its meaning to the congregation to show them how it should affect their daily lives.

imam The word 'imam' means literally 'the person who is imitated'. The imam stands slightly in front of the first row of worshippers to lead the prayers in a Muslim gathering. When choosing an imam, a community will always try to choose the person who is most honoured among them for his knowledge and understanding of the Qur'an and for living as a good Muslim. If necessary, any Muslim man can act as imam and lead the prayers.

How a mosque is used

'A place of prostration...'

The word for the third prayer position is **sajdah** which means 'prostration'. **Masjid** comes from the same Arabic word as sajdah and means 'place of prostration'. It is the place where Muslims show physically their willingness to submit to the will of God.

A mosque is meant primarily as a place of worship, but it is also much more than that. Because from the very earliest Islamic times, people met there five times each day, the mosque became an important community centre where discussions took place and decisions were made about community matters. Teaching and learning about the Qur'an and Islamic law also took place within the mosque, and still does today in many places. But whatever they are engaged in, people are still expected to remember that the mosque is a place of worship and to behave appropriately. Trading, shouting, talking during prayer times and doing anything which might offend other people are all forbidden in a mosque.

One of the companions of the Prophet Muhammad reported that he once said: '...for me the earth has been made a mosque and a means of purification; therefore if prayer overtakes any person of my community he should say his prayers wherever he is...' Prayer, not where it is said, is the important thing. Because

prayers can be said anywhere and so in one sense the whole world is a mosque, no consecration of the mosque is necessary. But once a mosque is built, it can never be used as anything else. It must always remain a mosque.

Decoration in a mosque

It is important to Muslims that the decoration of the mosque should help them to concentrate on their prayer and not be a distraction. Because of the importance of the Arabic language and the Qur'an, calligraphy often forms a significant element in the decoration of mosques. The calligraphic designs are intricate and beautiful. It does not matter that their complexity often makes them difficult to read even for an Arabic speaker, because they are meant more as examples of beauty and order than as texts to be read.

The symmetrical, arabesque and geometric designs which often decorate inside and outside walls of mosques, together with the calligraphic designs, help to express the Islamic belief in the oneness, eternity and infinity of God and the presence of God throughout the ever-repeating and interwoven patterns of the universe.

A place of prayer may be very simple or very splendid . . .

Fasting, festivals and food

Fasting

Ramadan is the ninth month of the Islamic calendar. In this month, Muslims do not eat or drink during the hours of daylight. Muslim children look forward to Ramadan with excitement because it is a special time. When they are very young, their parents do not allow them to fast because it would not be good for them. As they grow older, they will be allowed to join in a little more each year until by the age, usually, of about thirteen, they complete the whole month of fasting.

"I always like it when Ramadan is coming because there's a special feeling in our house and the sense of belonging to the family is very strong.

Each day in Ramadan, we wake up before sunrise and pray together and then we have something to eat before the fast starts. Then we don't eat or drink again until it's really dark. When Ramadan comes in the summer like it did this year, that means we fast for a very long time! Waiting all together in the evening to break the fast by having our evening meal is a nice time. When I was little, it was that time that made me want to join in with the fasting more than anything else, I think. The family evening meal was a really happy time and I thought I would enjoy the food more if I had managed to fast the whole day like the others. Anyway, when you are little you get a special treat if you fast! For instance your mum cooks your favourite food in the evening or something like that. When I was eight I asked my mum if I could fast. She wouldn't let me do more than one day. I did my first whole month when I was twelve. You feel really important and grown up and part of the family."

"When I was little, I didn't really think about why we fast until one of my friends at school asked me about it. They thought it was strange I didn't have dinner or eat at playtime. I think they actually felt a bit sorry for me which was funny because I was feeling very proud about it! I asked my mum why and she said we do it because it is a duty for Muslims. It's for self discipline and also so that we can understand what hungry people feel like."

The calendar

'When Ramadan comes in summer... we fast for a very long time!'

Each of the twelve months of the Islamic calendar has either 29 or 30 days and begins with the sighting of the new moon (so of course, days 'begin' not at midnight but just after sunset, which is why the first prayer of the day is the maghreb prayer). Therefore the lunar year on which all religious observances in Islam are based has 354 days and is eleven days shorter than the solar year (twelve days in a leap year). This means that Ramadan (and the other important occasions in the Islamic calendar) move gradually 'backwards' through summer, spring, winter and autumn. So Muslims in Britain will sometimes be fasting during long summer days and sometimes during short winter days. In countries near to the equator, of course, there is much less variation in the length of days.

Here are the names of the months in the Islamic calendar:

Muharram	Jumada-ul-Awwal	Ramadan
Safar	Jumada-ul-Akhir	Shawwal
Rabi-ul-Awwal	Rajab	Dhul-Quaada
Rabi-ul-Akhir	Shaban	Dhul-Hijja

These names date back to pre-Islamic times in Arabia, but in those days a month was added to the calendar every third year so that the lunar calendar kept up with the solar year. It is said that the Prophet Muhammad insisted on the change to the lunar year.

'He (Allah) it is who appointed the sun a splendour and the moon a light, and measured for her stages, that ye might know the number of years and the reckoning...' (10:5)

---

1. Look at a newspaper which shows the times of dawn and dusk. How many hours would a Muslim have to fast today, if it were Ramadan now?
2. Use a calendar of religious festivals to find out when Ramadan begins this year, according to the Christian Era calendar. Make a chart to show the dates of Ramadan for the next five years.
3. Here are four important dates in the Islamic calendar: 1st Muharram, 10th Muharram, 12th Rabi-ul-Awwal, 27th Ramadan. Find out why these dates are important to Muslims.

Why Muslims fast

'We do it because it's a duty for Muslims...'

Muslim children are taught that fasting in Ramadan is first and foremost an act of obedience to God, because the Qur'an commands Muslims to observe the fast. They will probably have read the command (2:183–187) in mosque school.

There are other benefits for people who fast, which children gradually come to understand as they join more and more in the fasting with their families. They learn that it is good for people to be self disciplined and to be able to control their natural desires. It is good for people who normally have more than enough to eat to feel what it is like to be hungry. It will help children later on to understand the importance of sharing what they have with the needy (⟶ page 54).

There is also a great sense of community created by the fast. Children understand this first of all in relation to their own family, as you can see from the interview on page 26. But as they get older, they will understand that they are sharing the experience of the fast not just with their immediate family, but with the whole Muslim world.

'Oh you who believe! fasting is ordained for you as it was ordained for those before you, so that you may remain conscious of God.' (2:183)

Exemptions from fasting

'...it wouldn't be good for me...'

Since fasting is supposed to benefit the people who do it, there are obviously some groups of people who should not fast. Young children, much as they may want to join in, will be allowed by their parents to fast only for short periods until they are strong enough to undertake the full fast. People who are ill are allowed to eat in Ramadan and to make up the days of fasting when they are better. Women who are pregnant and those who have just had babies do not have to fast, and neither do very old people. People who are on long journeys may break the fast if keeping it is difficult for them. Any days which are missed should be made up before the next Ramadan. There is more detailed information about these exemptions in books of hadiths.

> Fasting in the hours of daylight in Ramadan is one of the five most important duties of a Muslim.

"Each day in Ramadan, we get together to read the Qur'an. We read a bit each evening until by the end of the month, we have read the whole Qur'an through once. It's not just us, a lot of people try to do this. People also try very hard to keep to the prayer times, to avoid arguing with people, to keep promises and so on. It's a time for making a real effort to live according to Islam."

Lailat-al-Qadr

As well as being the month of fasting, Ramadan is special for another reason. It was one night during Ramadan that the Prophet Muhammad received his first revelation from the Angel Gabriel. This night is called in the Qur'an, 'Lailat-al-Qadr', the Night of Power (97:1–5). The exact date is not known, but in the hadiths it is said to be one of the last ten nights of Ramadan and many Muslims celebrate it on the 27th of Ramadan by reading the Qur'an and by saying special prayers.

The festival of Eid-al-Fitr

When the new moon that signals the end of Ramadan and the beginning of Shawwal is sighted, the fast is over. On the 1st of Shawwal, Muslims all over the world celebrate one of the two major festivals of the year, Eid-al-Fitr, 'the festival of breaking the fast'. On this day, it is positively forbidden to fast. Special food is cooked and families celebrate together, giving presents and visiting friends and relatives. People are celebrating because they have fulfilled a very important and difficult obligation by completing their month's fast.

"I think older people sometimes feel a bit sad because Ramadan is over. They've come through something, and now it's over. It's a sort of sad and happy feeling at the same time."

Waiting for the new moon that signals the end of the fast and the beginning of Eid is an exciting time. News of the first sighting of the new moon, usually from one of the North African countries, is telephoned to embassies around the world. Local Islamic communities can then telephone a central information point to find out whether the fast is over.

*"When I lived in London, where the big mosque has facilities for men and women, we all went to the mosque. We would get up, clean the house from top to bottom, have a bath, put on our best, fine clothes and go to the mosque for Eid prayer. It was nice to see all the different styles of clothes from all the different cultural backgrounds, because there were Muslims from all over the world there. But everyone was wearing their best. There were thousands of people and it was really crowded. In the women's section at the mosque, everyone was so happy, hugging each other and saying '**Eid mubarak**'. You make lots of new friends."*

Muslims in Britain preparing food for Eid-al-Fitr.

"At home I used to help my mother prepare all kinds of sweets and special food during the last two or three days of the fast. It used to make my mouth water. My nan used to come round and help too. What sort of food you have at Eid depends on which culture you come from. In our house we eat pillao, which is rice with meat in it and my sister makes a special pudding which takes hours. It's got almonds and milk and lots of sugar in — it's lovely. We have the meal all together after Eid prayers at the mosque."

At Eid, Muslims often send greeting cards to friends and relatives who live too far away to be visited. They may have a quotation from the Qur'an on them or a picture of a famous mosque. Some have 'Eid mubarak' printed on them: عيد مبارك

Design and make an Eid card. You could use symmetrical, geometric or arabesque designs, and even try some calligraphy!

The festival of Eid-al-Adha

"My dad wrote a letter to the school so we could have the day off. It wouldn't have felt like a special day if we were at school. We would have missed everything."

The major festival of the Islamic year, Eid-al-Adha ('the feast of the sacrifice'), is celebrated by Muslims all over the world on 10th Dhul-Hijja, the month of the **hajj**. Children may accompany their parents to the special Eid prayers in the morning. They have new clothes for the festival and receive presents of money or books from relatives and friends. Many British Muslims give money to help feed the poor instead of buying an animal to sacrifice. In some cities, arrangements are made for those Muslims who wish to do so to have an animal sacrificed according to Islamic law at an abattoir. For pilgrims in Makkah, the festival is just one of the observances of the hajj, but one which is shared with them by all other Muslims wherever they are. So to understand the significance of the festival for Muslims, it is necessary to know something about the hajj itself, and what the pilgrims do when they make their pilgrimage to Makkah and the holy places nearby.

Going to Makkah

"The year we went to Makkah, hajj was at the end of July. Makkah was incredibly crowded. Hundreds of thousands of Muslims from all over the world come to make the pilgrimage, you know. My mum and dad had been on hajj once before, so they knew what to expect! It's a duty for every Muslim to go on hajj at the right time at least once in their lifetime, if it is at all possible for them, and a lot of people go more than once.

First we landed at Jeddah airport. When we stepped out through the airport doors, I couldn't believe it. The heat was amazing. It hit us like a wall. I thought what it must be like to fast in that kind of heat. We went to put on **ihram** *and then we went to Makkah by taxi. My brother and I were really excited. We were just dying to see the Ka'aba. We saw the arches of the mosque and we kept looking through trying to get a glimpse. My dad said 'Not yet, not yet. First we've got to put our luggage at the hotel'.*

Then finally we went to the Ka'aba and did **tawaf** *and* **sa'y**. *When you go there, it's really something wonderful, it's so satisfying. I kept thinking about all these people we heard about at mosque school, Prophet* **Ibrahim**, *Prophet* **Isma'il** *and especially Prophet Muhammad. When you realise that you are walking where they walked, it's really something special. And when you hear the call to prayer in these places, you feel as if the whole world is praying with you."*

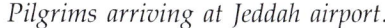

Pilgrims arriving at Jeddah airport.

The importance of the hajj

'...it's a duty for every Muslim to go on hajj at the right time at least once in their lifetime if it is at all possible for them...'

Even when they are very young, Muslim children will begin to learn about the hajj and its importance to Muslims. They will almost certainly see pictures of the Ka'aba in Makkah in their own homes, at the mosque and even on stamps from Muslim countries. They will be told the stories about Prophet Ibrahim, his wife **Haajar** and their son Isma'il whose actions are remembered in some of the observances of the hajj. They will hear stories from their own parents or from relatives returning from the hajj about their experiences in Makkah. Many Muslims spend years saving up enough money to go on the pilgrimage. When they return, they may use the title **Hajji** (**Hajja** for women) in front of their name to show that they have completed the hajj.

It is not a duty for people to go on the hajj if they genuinely cannot afford to, or if others would be harmed by their leaving. In Islam, actions are judged by intentions and there is a story about the hajj which is sometimes told to Muslim children to help them understand this.

A story about the hajj

An old man and his wife, knowing that a hajj accepted by God erases all sins, had saved money for many years so that they would be able to make the journey once before they died. On the night before they were due to leave for Makkah, they went to visit a neighbour they had not seen for some time. They found her very poor with not even enough money to buy sufficient food. So they gave all the money they had saved to their neighbour and returned home knowing that now they would never be able to go on the hajj.

But that night the angels were talking, saying that because the couple had really intended to make the pilgrimage and had not been able to because of their act of kindness to their neighbour, God had accepted their hajj as completed and their sins were forgiven.

Hajj observances

Ihram

Before approaching Makkah, pilgrims take a bath, or perform wudu and then they put on special clothes. Women and girls wear plain, long dresses with long sleeves and scarves to cover their hair. Men and boys use two large unsewn pieces of white material, one wound around to cover them from waist to ankles and the other over their shoulders. Children will be taught that these clothes are meant as a sign that the person wearing them has forgotten all about worldly things and is ready to think not about his or her own needs and desires but only about the will of God. So the word 'ihram' describes much more than just the clothes the pilgrims wear. It refers to the state of physical and mental readiness to submit to God's will.

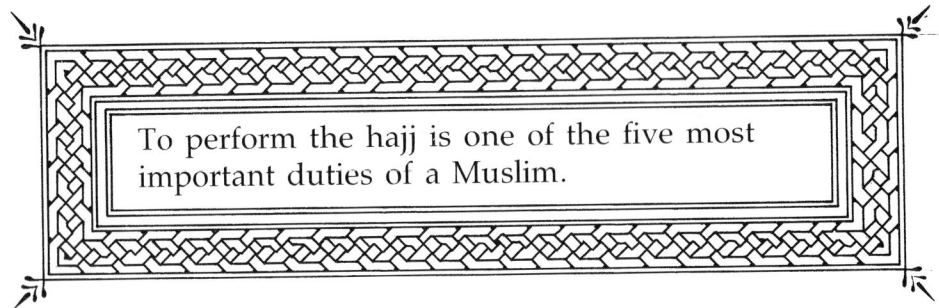

To perform the hajj is one of the five most important duties of a Muslim.

'...then we went to the Ka'aba and did tawaf and sa'y.'

As they read through the Qur'an, Muslim children will find references to the Ka'aba (e.g. 22:26, 2:127, 14:35). They will learn that it was built by Abraham and his son Ishmael as a place to worship the one God at a time when most people still worshipped idols. So, the children learn, the Ka'aba was really the first mosque to be built on earth, and Abraham, like all prophets before and after him, was trying to teach people that they should worship only the one God.

Tawaf

The Ka'aba stands in the courtyard of the Great Mosque, which was built around it. The pilgrims, wearing ihram, enter the courtyard and walk seven times around the Ka'aba reciting prayers as they go. On each circuit, they raise their hand towards the Black Stone set into the eastern corner of the Ka'aba. If they are close enough, they will touch or kiss the stone. This circling of the Ka'aba is called 'tawaf'.

The Ka'aba has been rebuilt several times, but the Black Stone is said to be part of the original structure built by Abraham. Because of this, it was specially venerated by the Prophet Muhammad whose custom (sunnah) it was to raise his hand towards it. Muslims today in saluting the stone, are following this custom.

Part of the **kiswah**, *the cloth that covers the Ka'aba.*

> 1 Ka'aba means 'a cube'.
> 2 The Ka'aba in Makkah is built of stone. It is about 14 metres high, 10 metres wide and 15 metres long.
> 3 It is usually covered in a black cloth embroidered in gold with verses from the Qur'an. This cloth is called the kiswah.
> 4 The Ka'aba is venerated by Muslims because of its historical associations, but it is certainly not worshipped. Muslims feel a great sense of **barakah**, grace or blessings, when they are near the Ka'aba, as it is a place that has been filled with people's prayers for 1400 years.

Sa'y

Sa'y is the next stage in the hajj observances. Pilgrims walk quickly seven times between two small hills in Makkah known as as-Safa and al-Marwa. They do this to commemorate Hagar's search for water for her son, Ishmael. Muslim children will be told the story of this event.

The story of Haajar and Isma'il

Haajar and Isma'il were in the desert near Makkah and had used up their supply of food and water. The heat of the desert was intense and Isma'il soon became very thirsty. Haajar desperately rushed from as-Safa to al-Marwa to see if she could find water for her son. When she returned to Isma'il, who by this time was near to death, she saw that in the spot where he had dug his heels into the ground, a spring was welling up. She gave him water from this spring to drink, and his life was saved. The spring is now known as the Well of Zamzam and pilgrims still drink from it today.

There is a version of this story in the Jewish and Christian scriptures.

After completing tawaf and sa'y, the pilgrims walk to the valley of Mina just outside Makkah and spend the first night of the hajj, the 8th of Dhul-Hijja, camped there.

In the next stages of the hajj observances, Muslims remember especially the story below about the Prophet Abraham. It is a story that all Muslim children will be familiar with.

Pilgrims go on the hajj in a spirit of total sacrifice. For the period of the hajj, they are giving up many things which are important to them – their comforts and pleasures, the companionship of friends and relatives, their pride and their status in society, because no one can tell who is rich and who is poor, who is important and who is not when everyone is dressed identically. And they are all doing this because they believe it is the will of God that they should. The story of Abraham's readiness to sacrifice what was most dear to him, his son Ishmael, because he believed God had commanded him to, is, for Muslims, one of the greatest examples of submission to God. This is the meaning of the story for Muslim children and when, as adults, they go on the hajj, the story will help them to remember the purpose of the hajj observances – that people should obediently do what God asks of them in his revelations. Here is a version of the story taken from a book written especially for Muslim children.

Ibrahim's great test

Ibrahim had to endure a great test. An angel came to him and said, 'You have to sacrifice your only son'. Ibrahim became very sad at this, but all the same, he knew that Allah had given him an order and he had to obey it. But first of all, he asked his son if he would agree. The son was good and pious and he consoled his father. 'Dear father,' he said calmly, 'if Allah has ordered it, then you must obey, so sacrifice me. Do not fear, with the help of Allah, I shall be brave.'

So, full of sorrow, Ibrahim prepared to kill his son. But before he actually did so, he heard a voice. 'You have shown your good intentions,' the voice told Ibrahim. 'This is sufficient. You have already fulfilled Allah's will.'

Thus Ibrahim's son was saved, and Ibrahim understood that Allah had been testing him. Of course Ibrahim was overcome with joy that he would not have to kill his son. They both thanked Allah and sacrificed instead an animal, as Allah had ordered.

To remember this occasion, we Muslims celebrate every year and like Ibrahim and his son, we sacrifice an animal. This reminds us that Allah put Ibrahim to a test to see whether he would really obey Him. Prophet Ibrahim passed the test and we celebrate in remembrance of this. Like Prophet Ibrahim, we also share the meat of the sacrificed animal with poor people and our friends. On this occasion, we also thank Allah for everything that He has given us and for the lesson He taught us through the rescue of Ibrahim's son.

Arafat and Muzdalifah

On the second day of the hajj observances, the 9th of Dhul-Hijja, the pilgrims travel either in vehicles or on foot towards Mount Arafat, where the Prophet Muhammad gave his farewell talk to the Muslims and where, according to tradition, Abraham took Ishmael to be sacrificed. It is about ten miles from Makkah. There, on the hot, dusty plain of Arafat hundreds of thousands of Muslim men and women and children join in zhur and asr prayers and spend the day asking God's forgiveness. This is the most important of the hajj observances when the sense of shared purpose is at its strongest. After sunset the pilgrims move on to Muzdalifah, where they say maghreb and isha prayers and camp for the night.

"As far as I could see, covering all the hills in the moonlight, were pilgrims from all over the world, all dressed in clothing not different from shrouds. For me, it was like a glimpse of the last judgement, when all people are gathered together, with no outward distinctions, to be judged by their actions in life."

Mina

On the next day, the 10th of Dhul-Hijja, the pilgrims celebrate the last of the hajj requirements, Eid-al-Adha, the 'feast of the sacrifice'. But first, early in the morning they leave Muzdalifah and move back to Mina. In the village there are three stone pillars. These represent the place where, traditionally, Shaytan, the devil, tried three times to tempt Abraham to disobey God's command to sacrifice Ishmael. To remember how Abraham overcame that temptation, the pilgrims throw stones at the pillars. They are 'fighting off the devil' and showing symbolically that they understand that everybody is tempted at some time to disobey God's will and must fight hard to ward off the temptation.

Young men picking up stones to throw at the pillars.

1 Read the account of Abraham's test in the Qur'an, 37:100−107. (You could also read the version of the story in the Bible, Genesis 22:1−18.)

2 "...the lesson he taught us through the rescue of Ibrahim's son..." What is the lesson that Muslim children learn from this story?

Eid-al-Adha at Mina

After communal prayers and the stoning of the pillars, most pilgrims sacrifice an animal, usually a sheep, a goat, or a camel. They do this to remember Abraham's willingness to sacrifice Ishmael and his sacrifice of a ram after Ishmael had been spared. As the animals are killed, the prayer 'Bismillah, Allahu-akbar' ('in the name of God, God is most great'), is said over them to show that the life is being taken only with God's permission and in order to provide food. Life is not being thoughtlessly destroyed. The animal will have its throat cut with a razor-sharp knife so that it feels nothing. The blood, which should not be eaten, will be allowed to drain away. Some of the meat will be eaten and the rest will be shared out among the poor.

The pilgrims may stay at Mina for two or three days after Eid-al-Adha, then go back to Makkah where they make a final circuit of the Ka'aba before returning to their own countries. When the obligatory hajj requirements are completed many pilgrims visit Masjid al-Nabawi, the Prophet's mosque and tomb, in Medina before leaving. Some even go to Masjid al-Aqsa ('the farthest mosque') in Jerusalem.

> Summarise the main observances of the hajj. Explain what happens and what the meaning of the event is for Muslims. Use the following headings: (1) Ihram, (2) Tawaf, (3) Sa'y, (4) Arafat and Muzdalifah, (5) Mina, (6) Eid-al-Adha.

Umra

*"At the proper time for hajj, Makkah is really packed with people. My mum and dad thought it would be better for us to see the holy places for the first time when there were less people around, so we did **umra**. I shall have to go again when I'm older, though, if I can, because just umra isn't enough."*

Muslims may, of course, visit Makkah at any time of the year for umra, the minor pilgrimage. For umra, they put on ihram and perform tawaf and sa'y just as they would for the hajj. Ihram is then taken off and umra is complete. But umra is not a substitute for the hajj, so Muslims who have completed umra should still perform the complete hajj at some time in their life if it is possible for them to do so.

Food laws

Halal and haram

*"When I first went to school, I had school dinners and I knew I couldn't eat the meat. I knew I had to have **halal** food, but I didn't know why. Then when I got a bit older, I started to find out about it partly from talking to my mum and partly from reading the Qur'an at mosque school. It says in the Qur'an what food is halal and what is **haram**. Actually, I don't like even touching non-halal meat because the habit of thinking about halal and haram in food is so ingrained in me. But in the Qur'an, it says that if you are hungry and there is only non-halal meat it's all right to eat it, so one day I might have to!"*

Some local education authorities in areas of Britain where a lot of Muslims live, do provide halal meat for school dinners.

'You are forbidden carrion, blood, and the flesh of swine; also any flesh that is dedicated to any other than Allah. You are forbidden the flesh of strangled animals and of those beaten or gored to death; of those killed by a fall or mangled by beasts of prey (unless you make it clean by giving the death stroke yourselves); also of animals sacrificed to idols... He that is constrained by hunger to eat of what is forbidden, not intending to commit sin, will find Allah forgiving and merciful.' (5:3)

The passage quoted is just one of those in the Qur'an which offer guidance to Muslims about food and drink. Here are some of the others: 2:168, 7:31, 5:87, 5:96, 5:5, 5:90.

It is not only animals sacrificed for Eid-al-Adha which are killed in the special way described on page 41. All meat eaten by Muslims should come from animals killed in the way laid down by the Qur'an and described in more detail in the hadiths. Muslim children living in a country where most people are not Muslims may find it quite difficult sometimes to decide what is halal and what is haram. Many foods such as ice cream, biscuits, tinned soups and meat pies may contain lard which is forbidden because it comes from a pig.

1 Collect food labels from biscuits, tinned soups, etc. Read the lists of ingredients and sort the labels into sets of halal and haram foods. Display the sets, and write labels to explain them.

2 If your school serves school dinners, read the menus for the week. If you were a Muslim, is there at least one choice each day that you could eat? Prepare some menus that could be enjoyed by both Muslims and non-Muslims. (They need not all include meat.)

3 Read the passages in the Qur'an relating to food and find out what the Islamic view is about
   a) over-eating,
   b) eating fish,
   c) alcohol.

4 Why is it important for Muslims that the meat they eat should come from animals killed in the way described on page 41?

Rights and relationships

Relationships between men and women

Getting married

"I just assume I will get married when I'm older — I'm a Muslim and the Qur'an says that all Muslims should marry. I've been to lots of weddings. The first one I can remember was when I was about seven and one of my cousins was getting married. We had gone to the bride's house a lot for about three days before the wedding day to help get all the special food ready. It was quite exiting because lots of the family were arriving from various places for the wedding party and I saw some of my cousins who I had not seen for a long time.

On the wedding day we didn't go to the actual ceremony, but there was a big party afterwards at the bridegroom's house. There seemed to be hundreds of people there. It was a really warm evening so they had the party outside in the courtyard. People brought round big trays with food on and there were musicians playing. Some of the people in the women's group danced, but mostly people just talked a lot. The women all gathered together on one side, the bride was with them. The children had a great time — we just ran around all over the place playing games and everyone was being nice to us. I especially liked going near the bride because she looked really pretty.

I couldn't tell at first which one of the boys was the bridegroom and I had to ask my mum. I've been to a Christian wedding party since then and they pay a lot more attention to the two people who are actually getting married. With us, it's more like a party for everyone."

'We didn't go to the actual ceremony...'

The marriage ceremony is just the final step in the careful arrangements made by the two families of the bride and groom. It is a short ceremony which may take place anywhere, for example at the mosque or at the bride's house. The two people just state before witnesses their willingness to marry each other. It is not a religious ceremony, so there is no need for a religious leader to be present. Sometimes, however, there may be a khutbah before the ceremony, during which passages from the Qur'an will be read to remind the two people of their duties towards one another. After the ceremony, the people present may say a prayer for the success of the marriage.

'...the Qur'an says that all Muslims should marry.'

'And marry, those among you who are single...'(24:32)

'And He it is who hath created man from water, and hath appointed for him kindred by blood and kindred by marriage...'(25:54)

Arranged marriages

These are just two of many quotations from the Qur'an that show how important marriage is for Muslims. Children learn about the importance of marriage partly by reading the Qur'an and the hadith, but also just by seeing how things happen in their own family. They learn not only that all Muslims should marry, but that getting married is not to be taken lightly, because for Muslims, marriage is the basis of human society. Choosing a marriage partner, then, is too much of a responsibility to be left to a young person to deal with all alone. Most Muslim parents would see it as part of their responsibility to help their children in their choice of a marriage partner and many young Muslims accept it as normal and appropriate that their families should help them in this matter.

"I don't think that an arranged marriage is such a bad idea. It worked for my mum and it has worked for a lot of people in our community. In western cultures, there's a lot of emphasis on romantic alliances, whereas we think there's a lot of logic involved in choosing someone to marry. When I get married I am going to be linking my whole future and my children's future and in many ways my whole family's future to one person — I don't think I could bear the responsibility of getting it right all by myself. I would expect my family to help me."

'Oh people! Be careful of your duty to your Lord, Who created you from a single being and created its mate of the same kind and spread from these two many men and women; and be careful of your duty to Allah, by Whom you demand one of another your rights, and to the ties of relationship; surely Allah ever watches over you.' (4:1)

This is one of the excerpts from the Qur'an which may be read during the wedding khutbah.

Divorce

"There are a lot of strange ideas around among non-Muslims about the relationships between men and women, a lot of distortions. There's

the 'four wives' stereotype to start with. In Islam, one wife is the ideal. If people knew about all the details, they would see that having more than one wife is allowed only in certain circumstances and it's not an easy thing to do. Divorce in Islam is not as easy as some of my friends seem to think either — it's not just the man saying 'I divorce you' three times. If it came to a divorce, both the families would have been involved and everyone would have agreed to it."

Islamic dress

"When I first came to this school, I really minded some of the things people used to say about the way I dress. They just assumed that nobody could actually want to wear things like this and that someone was making me do it.

In the Qur'an it says that women and men should dress 'modestly' — it doesn't say exactly what clothes you should wear. I wear loose clothes and I usually have a scarf on when I go out. I wear these clothes because I choose to, not because anyone makes me. I want to be treated as a person and respected as a person, not turned into a sex-symbol like some women think they have to be. They see my way of dressing as a form of oppression, whereas we see it as a form of liberation!"

School girls in Islamic dress.

What parents should do for children

Whispering the adhan

"When my baby brother was born, my dad went to see him at the hospital as soon as he could, right after he was born and he whispered the adhan into his ear. I asked him why, because the baby couldn't understand what he was saying. My dad said it didn't matter — he said it is just important for the baby to hear the words which are the most special ones for Muslims before he hears any other words in this world. And then he put a bit of honey on the baby's tongue so that he will always think of nice things when he hears the adhan.

My grandmother told me that where she came from, babies were usually born at home, not in a hospital, but they still whispered the adhan in the baby's ear and then someone would go into the courtyard and proclaim the adhan loud so that the neighbours would know the baby was safely born and everyone would be happy. It's not just our family that do it you know. It's all Muslims. They all want their babies to hear the special words before anything else."

Teaching about Islam

"In a Muslim family we welcome the baby into the world with the words which, for us, best express what Islam is and what it stands for — we start the baby out in a Muslim way! Any mother will do her best to feed her children and clothe them and play with them — she will do these things without even thinking about them as a duty. But as a Muslim mother, I think I have an even more important job to do, and that is to pass on to my children all that I know about our religion so that they gradually come to understand the way of life we lead, which is Islam. I hope I can help them to understand how to live this life, which is a preparation for the life to come."

The roles of the mother and father

In Islam, bringing up children is considered a very important job within the family and as primarily the job of the mother. The father has to provide financially for his family, but it is the mother who is charged with the day-to-day responsibility of looking after and teaching the children. There are many hadiths which describe the mother's role in an Islamic family — she should be a good friend to her children, affectionate, generous and fair to all of them.

At the same time she should teach them about Islam. Islamic society recognises that bearing children and looking after them when they are little is no easy job and it imposes great strains on women, so women bringing up children have a high status in society. The different definitions of the responsibilities of a mother and father are one example of how the roles of men and women are seen in Islam as being different — equally important and complementing one another, but certainly not the same.

What children should do for parents

"There are some verses in the Qur'an that say how children should be kind to their parents and do what they say and look after them when they get old because they looked after us when we were little and couldn't do anything for ourselves. I can't really imagine my parents being very old, but my grandmother is very old and she lives with us. She can't walk very far, but she helps in the house and she does a lot of the cooking. She tells me stories, a lot of stories about when she was little. I wouldn't like her to go and live in a home or a hospital. It would feel very bad and she would be lonely. I would be too. She will live with us until she dies."

Respect and gratitude

As they grow up, Muslim children learn that gratitude towards their parents and especially towards their mother is a very important duty. In fact, service to parents is second only to service to God. Whether parents are Muslims or non-Muslims, easy or difficult to get along with, they must be treated not only with respect, but also with kindness. Many verses in the Qur'an refer to children's responsibilities towards their parents while they are alive, especially when they get old and weak. Verses from the Qur'an such as those opposite will be familiar to

Muslim children who have been to mosque school. They will also read hadiths which stress the importance of kindness and respect to parents.

One Muslim scholar, Al-Qurtubi, explains clearly why children should show gratitude to their parents. He says that '...you should be compassionate to them as they were to you, and befriend them as they did you, remembering that when you were an incapable needy child, they preferred you to themselves, and they stayed awake nights, and went hungry while they satisfied your appetite, and were in need of clothes while they clothed you. So reward them when they reach old age in the condition that you were in as a child, in that you treat them as they did you, and give kindness to them priority.'

---

1 Why is there such an emphasis in Islam on showing respect for parents?
2 Why do Muslim families try so hard to look after elderly relatives at home rather than letting them go to an old people's home?

Some verses from the Qur'an that refer to 'parents' rights'

1 'Worship none save Allah only and be good to parents.' (2:83)

2 'Give thanks to me and unto thy parents.' (31:14)

3 'And show kindness unto parents and to kinsfolk and orphans and the needy.' (4:36)

4 'The Lord has decreed that ye worship none but him and that ye show kindness to parents. If one of them or both of them attain old age with thee, say not "Fie" to them or rebuke them, but speak to them graciously. And lower unto them the wing of submission through mercy and say: My lord! Have mercy on them both as they did care for me when I was little.' (17:23–24)

'...say not "Fie" to them...'
What kind of behaviour do you think this is 'shorthand' for?

Death and after

'Surely we belong to God and surely we return to Him.' (2:156)

Even after the death of parents, there are things that their children can do for them, as the following hadith shows:

'A man came ... and he said: Oh messenger of Allah, is there any remaining chance to show devotion to my parents after they have died? He said: Yes, prayer for them and asking forgiveness for them and the fulfilment of their contracts after them and the keeping up of family relations that they used to maintain and the respecting of their friends.' (Abu Dawud)

Death and burial

"They phoned us from the hospital to tell us that my grandad had died. I was really shocked — it was the first time that someone in my close family had died. After they phoned, the first thing we did was to say the special prayer from the Qur'an. It's sort of saying that you shouldn't grieve too much for the dead person because he has left the earth and gone back to God. That's what my dad told us — it was his dad who died. I cried anyway because I couldn't help it but I was crying because I felt I had lost someone. I was crying for me really, not for him. My dad still goes to the grave sometimes to say prayers."

When a Muslim is close to dying, those with the dying person will try to get him or her to say the Shahada. Just as they are some of the first words whispered to a newborn baby, so they should be the last words a Muslim says in this world.

After the person has died, the body will be covered with a cloth, washed — discreetly, as if the person were still alive — and wrapped in a shroud. This will usually all be done by members of the family — the body is not sent out to a funeral home. Muslims prefer burial to take place as soon as possible, usually within twenty-four hours. The body is not put into a coffin, but straight into the grave, the face turned towards Makkah. The special burial service is said, to ask forgiveness for the dead person, then friends and relatives will usually gather to console the bereaved family.

A Muslim woman speaks:

"I helped my mother to wash my aunt when she had just died. I thought it was going to be an awful thing to do but it wasn't. We had loved her when she was alive and this was just the last thing we could do for her. Somehow it made it easier for me to accept that she was really dead. Also, while we were washing her I kept thinking that one day I will be dead too, and someone will do that for me."

Paradise

The Qur'an says that on the Day of Judgement the Archangel Asrafil will sound the trumpet to raise the dead. Those who have struggled to live according to God's law will enter paradise and those who have not will find themselves in hell.

The Qur'an describes paradise as a wonderful garden with streams of cool water flowing through it, where the faithful will live for ever in ease and comfort and will finally see God (e.g. 2:25, 43:70ff, 76:12ff).

Gardens are very important in Islamic cultures. In hot climates, to walk beside flowing water in the shade of trees and to smell the scent of flowers in the air is an experience people appreciate very much. Formal gardens are tended with great care.

The garden of paradise is often symbolically represented in the design of fine Persian carpets. This carpet design shows streams, fish, trees and shrubs.

"I don't necessarily believe that paradise is exactly a garden. I believe that God used those words to describe it because those were the words that would help people to understand what it would be like. The image of a cool and beautiful garden would give them the feeling of the beauty of paradise and a longing for it."

Relationships with the wider community

*"When I was little, I wasn't really aware of our family paying **zakat**. I just knew that we gave some money each year to send to poorer people than us but I didn't know the proper rules about it until I was much older. I learned about **zakat-al-fitr** first because I actually saw it being collected at the mosque. That's the extra zakat they collect before the Eid prayers at the end of Ramadan, so that people who couldn't afford to have a feast for Eid without help can afford to have one. But that's separate from the main zakat payment."*

Zakat

Islam stresses that as well as having a responsibility towards their immediate family, Muslims who are financially able to do so have a duty to help people in the community who are in need. One way of doing this is by paying zakat. Zakat is a hard word to put into English. Sometimes it is translated as 'charity' but there is another word for that, **sadaqah**, which has a different meaning for Muslims. Zakat is a religious duty laid down in the Qur'an. Prayer and zakat are often mentioned in the same verse. It is an obligation on all Muslims to give a percentage of their savings each year in money or goods to be distributed to those who need it more than themselves. Muslims who have no savings of course do not have to pay zakat. In fact, it is their right, if they are too poor to meet all the necessary expenses of housing, food, clothing, education and other essentials for their own families, to receive money to help them to do so from the zakat paid by others. In an Islamic country the government may collect and distribute zakat, but in other countries, it is up to each individual man and woman to assess how much they should give, and to distribute the zakat.

The literal meaning of zakat is 'purity'. Paying zakat 'purifies' the rest of what a person has, because it reminds the human owner of the belief that God who created everything is also the owner of everything. All that the world produces, including wealth, should be used in a way pleasing to God. Money is only 'on loan' to people and God has given them the responsibility of using it properly.

'...righteous is the person who believes in Allah...and gives wealth, for love of Him, to kinsfolk and orphans and the needy and the wayfarer and those who ask, and sets slaves free; and observes proper worship and pays zakat...' (2:177)

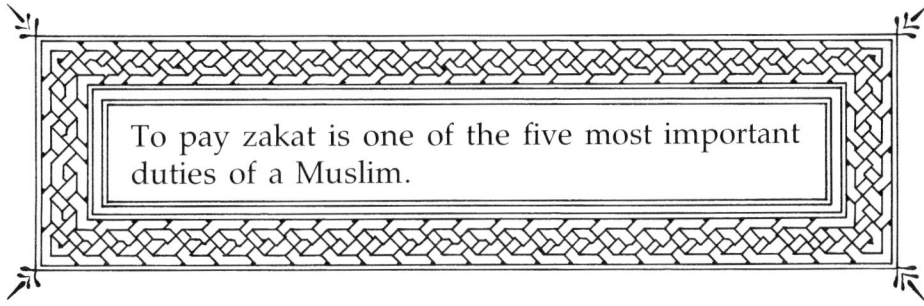

To pay zakat is one of the five most important duties of a Muslim.

Sadaqah

Sadaqah, charity, is voluntary, not a duty. All kinds of good deeds, not just the giving of money, count as sadaqah. Kindness to animals, cleaning rubbish from a roadway where it could be dangerous to travellers, planting a tree — all these things are described in the hadiths as 'charity'. Children growing up in a Muslim family will learn that quite small acts of kindness and thoughtfulness can be important and meaningful if they are done in a truly Islamic spirit. Even keeping a cheerful expression when you are feeling fed up can be sadaqah!

'The messenger of Allah said: Every good deed is charity, and it is a good deed that thou meet thy brother with a cheerful countenance and that thou pour water from thy bucket into the vessel of thy brother.' (*Musnad* of Ahmad)

Relationships with the natural world

"We can use anything we like from the world — that's what it's there for, that's what Allah made it for. But people should take care of the world because really it belongs to Allah, the land, all the animals and birds — everything in the world. Whatever we do, we should know that. That's why we eat halal meat, for instance, because when the animal was sacrificed, it had a prayer said over it to show that the person who took its life knew that it was Allah's creature and he was only killing it for food, not for fun or for no reason at all. We should share with other people too, food, money, whatever we have, because Allah made the things for everyone, not just for the people who have the money to buy them.

There are lots of stories from Prophet Muhammad's times about the earth and birds and animals and treating them well — even looking after trees. I've got some of them in books at home."

Muslims believe that God created the whole universe including the Earth and all its resources. Because God created people with the power to reason, they have a great responsibility to use what the world produces carefully and not selfishly or wastefully. They are looking after the world on God's behalf and are accountable to God for their use of its resources. These ideas of trusteeship, **khalifah**, and accountabilty to God, **akhra**, are two of the central ideas in Islam.

'Let man consider his food: how we pour water in showers and split the Earth in clefts and cause the grain to grow therein and grapes and green grass and olives and dates and enclosed gardens dense with trees and fruit and fodder, provision for you and your cattle,' (80:24–32)

A formal Islamic garden at Kashan, Iran. Look back at the design of the carpet on page 53 and compare it with the design of the garden. Can you see the similarities?

Living a Muslim life

In this book you have been finding out how Muslim children learn about Islam and what it means to live a Muslim life. Some things can be taught to them directly, first at home, by their mother and other members of their family, later at mosque school. They can learn, for instance, about the five important practical ways in which a Muslim demonstrates his obedience to God. These duties, all laid down in the Qur'an, are known as the five 'pillars' of Islam. Look through the book and you will find them highlighted within the text.

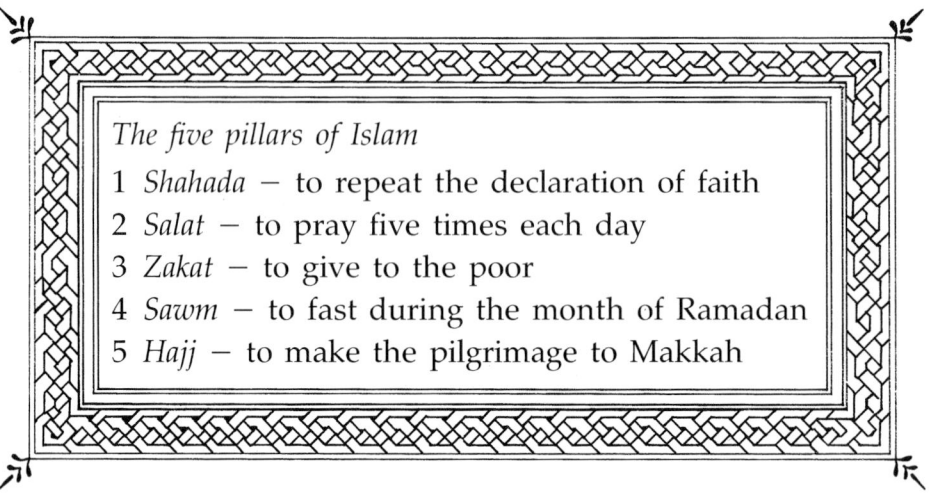

The five pillars of Islam
1 *Shahada* — to repeat the declaration of faith
2 *Salat* — to pray five times each day
3 *Zakat* — to give to the poor
4 *Sawm* — to fast during the month of Ramadan
5 *Hajj* — to make the pilgrimage to Makkah

But having read the book, you will understand that knowing about these things is only part of learning to live as a Muslim. Children's deeper understanding of what it means to be a Muslim comes from belonging to a Muslim community. Gradually, as they grow up within a Muslim family, children become aware that Islam is a religion which affects every aspect of their daily lives.

As their understanding of Islam slowly increases, children accept more and more responsibility for their own actions and by the time they are thirteen or fourteen they will be expected to have learned and understood enough to be able to live a Muslim life. From then on it will be their own choice and their own responsibility to follow Islam — no one else is responsible for their actions.

These girls, who are wearing Islamic dress, are having a calligraphy lesson.

"It's sometimes hard to be a Muslim living in Britain, all the messages coming from the society are different. The basic values are different."

> What do you think this Muslim girl meant by "the messages coming from the society are different. The basic values are different."?
>
> Make a list of those aspects of British society that she might see as in conflict with the message of Islam.
>
> How would you explain what the basic values of Islam are?

60

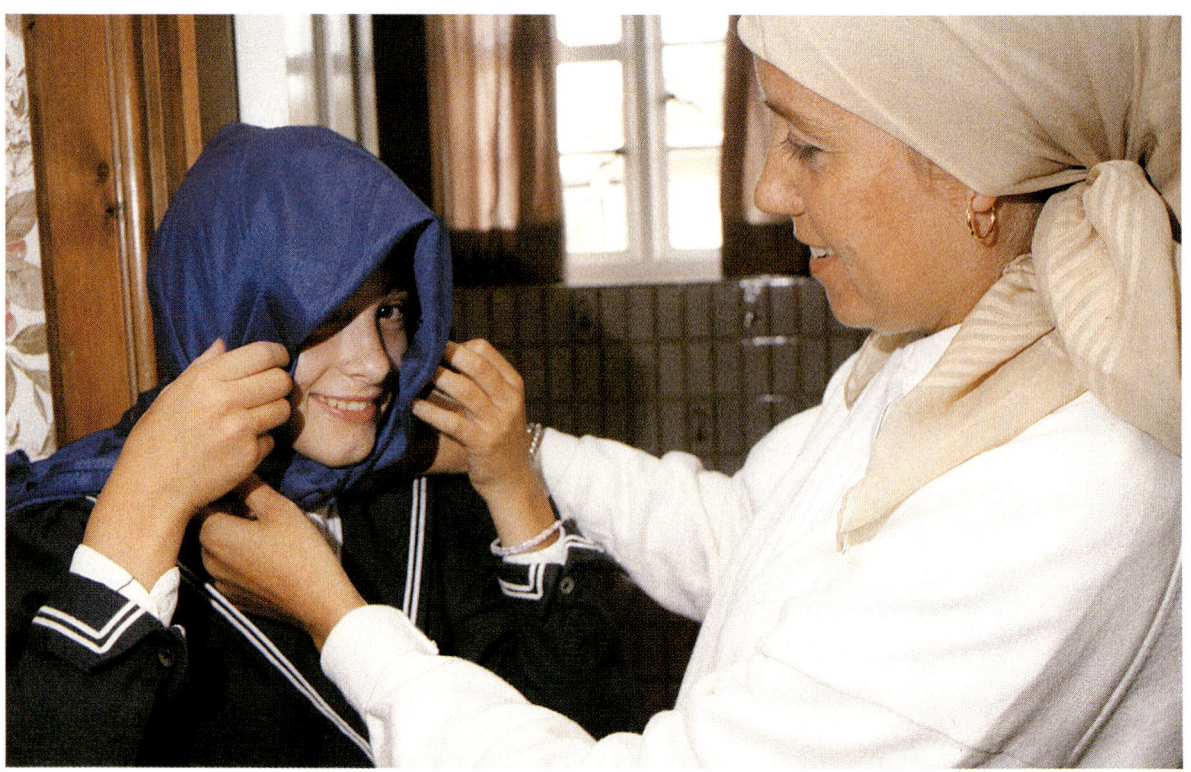

"Why do I live this way? Well first, it's the way I was brought up, so it's part of my thinking. But also, the more I follow Islam, the more I get a calm sort of feeling and the more I think it is the right way to live. It's hard to explain to someone who is not a Muslim, but Islam means submission to the will of God and Muslim means someone who has submitted to the will of God. I believe Islam shows the way God wants people to live. If you believe that, why would you want to live any other way?"

Glossary

Here are the meanings of the Arabic words used in this book.

adhan the call to prayer

akhra accountability to God

alhamdullillah 'praise be to God'

Allah God

asr mid afternoon, the name of the fifth prayer

assalamu aleykum the Islamic greeting, literally 'peace be with you'

ayah a verse of the Qur'an

barakah grace, blessings

bismillah 'in the name of God' – appears at the beginning of all the surahs in the Qur'an except one

Eid feast, festival

Eid mubarak 'blessed festival', a festival greeting

al-Fatihah 'The Opening', the title of the first surah of the Qur'an

fajr dawn, the name of the third prayer

fard obligatory

Haajar Hagar, wife of Abraham

hadith 'tradition', accounts of the sayings and actions of the Prophet Muhammad

Hafiz a person who has learned the Qur'an by heart

hajj the pilgrimage to Makkah

hajja a woman who has performed the pilgrimage to Makkah

hajji a man who has performed the pilgrimage to Makkah

Hijra 'migration', Muhammad's journey from Makkah to Medina in 622 CE

halal 'permitted'

haram 'prohibited'

Ibrahim Abraham, father of Ishmael

ihram the state of ritual purity, also the name for the special clothes worn by pilgrims on the Hajj

imam 'the one who is imitated', the man who leads the congregation in prayer

isha night, name of the second prayer

Islam 'submission' to the will of God

Isma'il Ishmael, son of Abraham and Hagar

jalsah 'sitting', one of the positions of prayer

Ka'aba 'cube', the shrine in the Great Mosque at Makkah

khalifah trusteeship

kiswah the embroidered cover of the Ka'aba

khutbah speech, sermon

maghreb evening, the name of the first prayer

masjid 'the place of prostration', a mosque

Masjid-al-Nawabi the Prophet's mosque and tomb, in Medina

mihrab the alcove in the wall of a mosque which indicates the direction of Makkah

minbar raised platform in a mosque from which the imam speaks at Friday prayers

mu'adhdhin the man who calls the adhan (sometimes written muezzin)

Nuh Noah

qibla direction of Makkah

qiyam 'standing', one of the positions of prayer

Qur'an the sacred text of Islam

rak'ah one unit of prayers

Ramadan the ninth month of the Islamic calendar, the month of fasting

ruku bowing of the head and body, one of the positions of prayer

sadaqah voluntary charity

sajdah 'prostration', one of the positions of prayer

salat ritual prayer

sawm fasting

sa'y moving between the hills of as-Safa and al-Marwa, one of the observances of the hajj

Shahada the declaration of faith

sunnah custom, tradition, the practice of the Prophet Muhammad

surah a chapter of the Qur'an

tawaf circling the Ka'aba, one of the observances of the hajj

tawheed divine unity

umra minor pilgrimage to Makkah

wudu ritual washing before prayer

zakat obligatory alms-giving

zakat-al-fitr additional zakat paid at the end of Ramadan

zhur noon, the name of the fourth prayer

Index

NB Words in the index refer to pages where the topic is discussed and not only to those where the actual words occur.

Abraham (see Ibrahim)
adhan 20, 22, 33, 48
Arabic language 5, 6–8, 10, 18–19, 24, 25

barakah 37
Bible (Jewish and Christian scriptures) 37, 40
burial 52

calendar 26–27
call to prayer (see adhan)
calligraphy 8, 25, 31
  examples of calligraphy 4, 8, 9, 22, 31, 36
charity (see sadaqah, zakat)

death 52–53
divorce 47

Eid 13
Eid-al-Adha 32, 40, 41
Eid-al-Fitr 30–31

fasting 26, 28–29
Fatihah 9, 17
five pillars of Islam 17, 20, 29, 34, 55, 58
food
  halal 41, 42–43
  haram 42
Friday prayers 13, 21

Haajar 33, 37
hadith 14, 28
  examples of hadiths 9, 13, 17, 24, 52, 55

Hafiz 5
Hagar (see Haajar)
hajj 32–41
  tawaf 33, 36
  sa'y 33, 37
  Arafat and Muzdalifah 39
  Mina 40–41
Hajja 33
Hajji 33

Ibrahim 10, 33, 36, 38
ihram 32, 34, 36, 38, 39
imam 23
Ishmael (see Isma'il)
Islamic dress 47, 59
Isma'il 33, 37, 38

Ka'aba 16, 22, 23, 32, 35–37
kiswah 36, 37

Lailat-al-Qadr 29

marriage 44–47
masjid 21–25
  decoration of a mosque 24
Masjid al-Aqsa 41
Masjid al-Nabawi 41
mihrab 23
minbar 23
mosque (see masjid)
mosque school 4–5, 28
mu'adhdhin 22
Muhammad 7, 8, 9, 10–11, 13, 14, 16, 17, 20, 24, 27, 29, 36, 39, 41, 56

Night of Power (see Lailat-al-Qadr)

paradise 53
pilgrimage (see hajj)
pilgrims' dress (see ihram)
prayer (see salat)
prayers in everyday speech 19

qibla 22, 23
Qur'an 4–5, 9, 10–11, 13, 17, 22, 24, 25, 28, 29, 31, 35, 40, 43, 44, 45, 46, 47, 50, 52, 53, 54, 58
  passages from Qur'an 9, 10, 20, 27, 28, 43, 46, 51, 55, 56

Ramadan 26, 27, 28–29, 30

salat 12–19
  prayer times 18
  prayer positions 16–17
  prayer rugs 16

sadaqah 54–55
Shahada 20

umra 41

wudu 14–15

zakat 54–55
zakat-al-fitr 55